1 25

D0824376

ADIRONDACK HIGH

ADIRONDACK HIGH

Images of America's First Wilderness

HARDIE TRUESDALE

Preface and Text by Joanne Michaels

Introduction by Elizabeth Folwell

◀ **Indian Lake Sunrise**

Most photographs of sunrises aren't
compelling—incorporating such
elements as clouds or mist may make
all the difference. This atmospheric
shot was taken from the western
shore of Indian Lake looking east.
I knew that it would be clear and cold
by Indian Lake while camping out the
previous night. The resulting dew and
moisture, along with the rising mist
during sunrise, made for an unusual
effect. The shoreline on the left side of
the photo is a dark, dramatic anchor in
contrast to the fiery light on the right.
The rest was luck!

THE COUNTRYMAN PRESS
WOODSTOCK, VERMONT

DEDICATION

To John Heard, my dear friend,
who has always been there for me. —J. M.

I would like to dedicate this book to my father, C. W. Truesdale,
and my mother, Joan Wurtele,
who always encouraged my creativity. —H. T.

Photographs copyright © 2005 by Hardie Truesdale
Text copyright © 2005 by Joanne Michaels
First Edition

All rights reserved. No part of this book may be reproduced in any way by any electronic or
mechanical means, including information storage and retrieval systems, without permission in
writing from the publisher, except by a reviewer, who may quote brief passages.

Library of Congress Cataloging-in-Publication Data has been applied for.

Book design and composition by Susan McClellan
Published by The Countryman Press, P.O. Box 748, Woodstock, Vermont 05091
Distributed by W. W. Norton & Company, Inc.,
500 Fifth Avenue, New York, New York 10110
Printed in Spain by Artes Graficas Toledo
10 9 8 7 6 5 4 3 2 1

CONTENTS

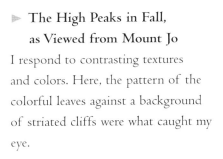 **The High Peaks in Fall, as Viewed from Mount Jo**
I respond to contrasting textures and colors. Here, the pattern of the colorful leaves against a background of striated cliffs were what caught my eye.

PREFACE

ADIRONDACK HIGH IS A CELEBRATION OF AMERICA'S FIRST WILDERNESS, the Adirondack Park, a patchwork of private and public lands, created in 1892, with the nation's largest trail system—more than 2,000 miles. Roughly the size of the state of Vermont, the park contains six million acres and has neither an entrance gate nor an admission fee. There are thousands of lakes, 1,800 miles of rivers, forty-six mountains of more than 4,000 feet in elevation, countless trees, and rare vegetation that thrives under adverse conditions.

Hardie Truesdale, a renowned nature photographer for more than thirty years, has brought together word and image to highlight some of the many places that make the Adirondacks so spectacular. With masterful use of light and texture, Truesdale captures the sublimity of the Adirondacks and some of its most compelling vistas. Unlike many photographers who shoot hundreds of photographs of their subjects, Truesdale works as a painter would, carefully seeking out each scene. He often resembles an animal stalking its prey, with a palpable energy about his movements as he searches for just the right shot. Once he has found it, and only then, does Truesdale relax and take the photograph . . . one, perhaps two shots. It is unusual for a photographer to so candidly share his thoughts and feelings as they are revealed here. Readers are in for a treat: a rare glimpse into what went on "behind the scenes" in obtaining each photograph.

Many photographers will be found outdoors when the light is perfect and the weather is sunny and clear. Truesdale heads out to work in blizzards, rainstorms, fog, and mist; such conditions enhance the mood of the wild environment by creating interesting light and shadows. In fact, he will hike for miles in a storm, and then wait on a mountain summit for hours in frigid cold until the clouds break and the mountains become visible in order to capture just one photograph to his satisfaction. His commitment, patience, and, ultimately, his vision are unique. The images are not just beautiful; they capture the spirit of the Adirondacks.

—Joanne Michaels

▶ **Fall Views, Marcy Dam**
What Grand Central Station is to New York City, this interior outpost is to Mount Marcy. Though thousands of hikers pass through or camp here on their way to hike the Adirondack High Peaks, you still find astonishing beauty, especially in the stillness of an early-fall morning.

ACKNOWLEDGMENTS

We are grateful to The Countryman Press, in particular, Kermit Hummel, who envisioned this book and got us started on the project, and Richard Fumosa, who edited the volume with excellence. And we'd also like to thank Susan McClellan for her outstanding design and layout.

HARDIE TRUESDALE

7

Introduction: In the Eyes of the Beholder

T HE ADIRONDACKS—THAT CURIOUS CORNER OF UPSTATE NEW YORK, RUMPLED with mountains and dotted with lakes, has always seemed a promised land. When the region became a state park in 1892, it offered all manner of strenuous sports as well as leisurely lounging. Today, hikers and climbers flock to the High Peaks, a gang of forty-six mountains towering over 4,000 feet, or tram the 134-mile Northville–Lake Placid Trail that traces a diagonal from remote southwestern ponds and old-growth forests toward the great ranges to the north. Kayakers and canoeists head for the backcountry lakes and miles of whitewater. Skiers look for the first flakes of snow and head out on trails that crisscross the dozen-plus wilderness areas. Anglers, bird-watchers, rock-climbers, snowshoers, trail runners, backpackers and hunters all claim their own favorite turf within the six-million-acre park.

That's our modern take on this place, a constitutionally protected Forest Preserve, with private land, too, about a hundred hamlets, crossroads, settlements, and villages. We do see the forests from the trees, though when we look out over still blue waters, thinking about the dams that created that waterway doesn't factor into the equation. The hand of man has made its mark, impressions colored by schemes and dreams. To speculators, its wide-open spaces offered incalculable profits; for loggers and miners, the forests and ore deposits appeared limitless. This was a place, midway between Montréal and Manhattan, ripe for the plucking.

Reality was different from these far-flung dreams, of course. The territory had seen battle after battle beginning in the 1750s, and even with armies discovering quiet valleys and strong-running streams, settlement was a tough proposition, with only a handful of towns arising along the shores of Lake Champlain. Once peace reigned in the new republic, real-estate schemers carved out huge parcels, hoping to capture buyers interested in cheap land in this up-and-coming state. But few wanted to give up hard-earned

▶ **Boulder in the Mist, Henderson Lake**

While walking on a trail along Henderson Lake, I became drawn to that solitary boulder. The contrast between the soft surface of the lake and the starkness of the rock made me stop. So, I ran back to the car for my camera and tripod. Though it was pouring, you can't see the rain falling in this photograph. I carried in two umbrellas and tarps, and pitched one umbrella over the camera and tripod. I had to hold my breath setting up the equipment so that the camera back wouldn't fog up. Then, I lined up the boulder in the narrows—off to one side, as I dislike to center images. The boulder, which anchors the photograph, is on the right, its blackness juxtaposed against the subtle colors of the lake. Rain and mist, which I often like to work with, technically assist in evoking the mood of wildness that is so much a part of the Adirondacks.

◀ **Views from Mount Marcy—**
Van Hoevenberg Trail

This photograph was taken from Little Marcy, one of Mount Marcy's several "false peaks," on a summer day, just after a rainstorm. The clouds had suddenly parted, exposing mountain views reminiscent of a lunar landscape. Being above the timberline is like being in another world. Some of the plants that grow there flourish nowhere else.

cash for a hardscrabble farm within a dire wilderness, when a clever farmer could go to the fertile Midwest and find better options.

Settling the middle of today's six-million-acre Adirondack Park did not really begin until the 1850s. The economy then included resource extraction—or exploitation; take your pick. Tanning hides for shoe leather built many an Adirondack hamlet, as hemlock trees and their tannin-rich bark were plentiful. Around each sprawling, stinking tannery was a clear-cut, where the enormous logs, stripped of their bark, were left to rot. Indeed, it was tall timber that attracted the first moneyed interests to the region, because monster white pines were tall and straight enough for the Royal Navy fleet's masts. Once those giants were felled, other softwoods followed, floating to market on rivers declared as public highways by the state legislature early in the nineteenth century.

Civilization depends on iron, and it happened the Adirondacks had—and still have—plenty. Ore was found in the southwestern Adirondacks (around a town named, fittingly, Old Forge), where mines and furnaces supplied the materials for the Brooklyn Bridge and the USS *Monitor*, the ironclad Civil War warship. Iron processing involved far more than digging and crushing rock; charcoal was necessary for the forges and blast furnaces. An acre of hardwood a day was required to run an average operation, and the stench of smoldering wood hung in the valleys already ringing with the sound of the trip-hammer.

All this industry paints a grim picture, like the worst Pacific Northwestern clear-cut combined with ravaged strip mines, such as in the Pacific Midwest or Tennessee. There's more to the Adirondack story than blustering commerce, and from the region's first impressions, the Adirondacks has always claimed a wild, untamed beauty. Upon visiting Lake George in 1791, Thomas Jefferson wrote that it was the ". . . most beautiful water I ever saw."

The craggy peaks, splendid waterfalls, and hidden glens were a promised land to an artist as early as the 1820s. In engravings marketed in Europe and America, the region's rare scenery found new eyes. By the time of the Civil War, painters from the Hudson River School were packed easel to easel in Keene Valley; and interior lakes attracted the brush and palette of English-born painter Arthur Fitzwilliam Tait, whose prints of animals and sportsmen for Currier & Ives became hugely popular. Winslow Homer sketched both the High Peaks and the upper Hudson River with austere grace. From these scenes city folk saw grand forests; wildlife, such as deer, bear, wolves, and moose; prim little villages; and that iconic figure, the Adirondack guide, ready to take his sport in search of wily trout or trophy game.

Photographers were the next wave of landscape artists. In fact, a pair of America's best-known early photographers had true North Country roots. Matthew Brady, who made the Civil War real to millions with his graphic battlefield shots, was born in Warren County on a farm near North Creek. William Henry Jackson, who traveled west with the Geological and Geographical Survey of the Territories in the 1860s, made his name as chronicler of the Union Pacific route. He was a Keeseville boy, and when the Delaware & Hudson Railroad asked him to return to his stomping grounds to show all the lovely places along its tracks, Jackson jumped at the chance. He made thousands of images, some of them panoramas three feet long, of Lake Placid and other hotspots.

BY FAR, THOUGH, THE MOST DEVOTED ADIRONDACK CAMERAMAN was Glens Falls–born Seneca Ray Stoddard. No mountain was too remote for him, no river too treacherous. He carried his view camera, glass plates, and portable darkroom to many remote and inaccessible places, and he also knew the verandahs and mezzanines of the region's grand hotels that were built in the Gilded Age, when the Adirondacks—despite black flies, 30-hour-average rail, stage, or steamer trips, and unpredictable weather—was as trendy as Newport or Saratoga Springs. Stoddard capitalized on his intimate knowledge of towns, stagecoach routes, train schedules, local guides, even livery stables, to build a thriving business founded on stereopticon views, postcards, guidebooks, maps, souvenir-view albums, and more. From 1870 to the dawn of the automobile age, Stoddard made the Adirondacks a known place.

Luckily for us in the 21st century, Stoddard knew the wilderness he portrayed was incredibly fragile. He saw firsthand the denuded forests, the miserable mining towns. For the unsettled reaches of the region he became a powerful advocate, pressing the state of New York to protect its incomparable wildlands. Through lantern slide shows and lectures, the photographer brought the beauty of the land to a public eager to save

▲ **Red-Bellied Woodpecker in the Snow**

it from despoilation. Stoddard was not the lone voice for the wilderness, of course, but his pictures were indeed worth a thousand words.

Today, when we can glimpse other galaxies, or the ocean floor, it seems improbable that a landscape so near millions of people can remain hidden. Hardie Truesdale's photographs bring that glimpse of a rare landscape to us, and it should come as no surprise that he relies on nineteenth-century technology to create the images in *Adirondack High.* He uses a cumbersome view camera, an elegant wooden box with movable bellows, along with a sturdy tripod and an assortment of lenses with leaf shutters. He loads sheet film into metal holders in his New Paltz, New York darkroom, and carries twenty or more of these to his locations. Each frame is carefully composed on the ground-glass screen in the back of the camera, as Hardie hunches under a lightproof cape. If you were to walk to Henderson Lake, a glorious body of water in the midst of the High Peaks, and find him under the cape, holding an umbrella over the lens to protect it from the fine drizzle that crystallizes a subtle palette, you'd wonder if you had stumbled onto Stoddard's ghost. In a way, you have.

ADIRONDACK HIGH

◄ Painted Fall Mountainside,
as viewed from Mount Jo

◄ **Chapel Pond Fall**

For this four-second exposure, I waited almost two hours for the leaves to settle. A continuous slight breeze on a lightly windy day may cause such a wait; I was also waiting for a minimum of ripples on the water. The pond makes a fine backdrop for the fall maples and birch trees.

► **Fallen Birch, Chapel Pond**

It was a rainy spring day at the end of May, and I was walking on a trail by Chapel Pond, when I came upon this scene. The stark birch tree draws the viewer into the photograph—it's what you focus on in the foreground. The whiteness of both the tree and the mist over the mountains makes for an intriguing contrast with the dark water and deep green of the forest. At one time there were many white birches around this lake. Many were destroyed in an enormous ice storm that devastated the East Coast in 1998.

◄ **Winter Stream—Chapel Pond Outlet**

► **Talus in a Snowstorm, Poke-O-Moonshine**
A popular place to climb due to its wonderful views of Lake Champlain and the High Peaks, the mountain boasts a fire tower that is still in use. The unusual name is derived from two Algonquin Indian words: *pohqui*, which means broken, and *moosie*, which means smooth, probably referring to the smooth rocks of the summit, and the broken rocks of the cliff (talus) on the east side of the mountain.

◀ First Light, Cascade Mountain Summit

I hiked three miles in darkness using a headlamp in order to arrive at the mountain summit by sunrise and take this shot. I thought I would have the entire place to myself, but was surprised to find a troop of Boy Scouts had arrived first.

I crave the open space found on mountain summits. In the East, summits provide the same feelings of expanse as the open landscape of the West. The woods are closed in; often, during the hike up a mountain you feel that closeness. At the summit, it's a welcome relief to take in the vastness and majesty of the wilderness. You feel as though you can look out forever. It amazes me that people will hike to a summit, stay just five minutes, turn around, and then go down. I prefer to spend time alone on summits, looking out over vast spaces of the natural world. It gives me a feeling of peacefulness.

▲ Pitchoff Mountain Summit

The texture of the granite and the
intriguing cracks in the rock both lead
your eye to the mountains in the distance

► High Peaks, as Seen from the
　 Ledges on Pitchoff Mountain

Such ledges as these are often overlooked
by hikers because they focus, for the most
part, on reaching the summit. But such
aeries offer spectacular views and
are some of my favorite places to visit
and photograph. This shot was taken in
the evening light.

◀ Maples and Moss, Heart Lake

When you take the time to stop and observe the natural landscape, beautiful patterns and details emerge from just about everywhere. Here, for example, the delicate leaves seem almost to float atop the moss.

▶ Blue Ledge in Autumn, the Hudson River

The Blue Ledge is a limestone cliff that towers above a broad pool in the Hudson. And I love this spot on the river . . . the way the colorful tree pops out from the rocks, and how it anchors the composition as well. An image of such a place gives me a sense of inner quiet and contentment. It perhaps may also help others escape from the concerns of their daily lives.

▲ Spring-like Fall

The subtle fall colors contrasted with some trees' spring-like pale green, as well as the dark green of coniferous trees.

▶ Lake Durant Sunset

After discovering a group of boulders to place in the foreground, I waited for sunset. The water's gold and magenta colors turned out to be particularly striking on this summer evening. The campgrounds at Lake Durant are in an ideal location—right on the lake shore, so I could work at my campsite.

◄ Tapestry of Spring, East River Trail, East Branch of the Ausable

One June day while I was walking along the East Branch of the Ausable River, these wildflowers—two little red mocassin flowers, surrounded by ferns and bunchberries—caught my attention. Bunchberries are common spring blossoms in the evergreen forests of the Adirondacks, just one of the many wildflowers that make woodland walks so enjoyable at this time of year.

► Falling Water, Rainbow Falls

This nearly 150-foot-high waterfall that pours into a huge moss-covered ravine is a spectacular sight on the trail to Gothics Mountain. In order to capture it, I perched on a mossy, vertical cliff. Just as I was shooting the photograph, I heard what sounded like an explosion, with a roar much louder than the thunder of the waterfall. It was a huge rock slide no more than 100 feet from the precarious spot where I stood. The serene feeling of the photo's composition is far from what I felt at the time when the photograph was taken.

▲ Mossy Logs, East River Trail

▲ False Hellebore Leaf Patterns,
East River Trail

▶ **Ground Cover, East River Trail**

A rainy spring day in June—the perfect time to take a hike in the Adirondacks—is a veritable feast for the senses, when many types of flowers are beginning to bloom. Raindrops collect on plant leaves, accenting the beauty of new growth. The air literally smells of spring: Spruce mingles with a natural potpourri of outdoor scents. Walking along the banks of the Ausable, the sound of the rushing river and its two waterfalls soothes and relaxes you. Then, at the end of the East River Trail, a short trail leads to the summit of Indian Head Mountain with its sweeping views of Ausable Lake. Standing on this cliff and looking at the lake surrounded by steep, rugged mountains is a wonderful climax to a hike filled with natural beauty.

◀ **View of Lower Ausable Lake from Indian Head Mountain**

Take the time to slow down and look around on a beautiful hike on a rainy day, and you'll find an array of delicate beauty: flowers, ground cover, Hobbit-like woods, showered boulders, intimate waterfalls. Here I followed the East Branch of the Ausable. Although the day was dreary when this shot was taken, the stormy sky and stillness of the lake—with a stunning view of Lower Ausable Lake and the Sawtooth Mountains—keep inviting you to see what lies beyond them.

▶ **Showy Trillium, East River Trail**

Trillium, also known as stinkpot, blooms around mid-June in the Adirondacks. It's a beautiful wildflower, and relies on carrion-eating insects for pollination; by emitting an odor that resembles the smell of decaying flesh, the flower lures insects to it, hence its other name.

◄ **Rainbow Falls**

► **Boulders and Falling Water,
Rainbow Falls**

I was hiking the trail to Beaver
Meadow Falls, which is one of the
many attractions along the East Branch
of the Ausable River. I noticed the
boulders, and loved the way they were
being showered upon at the base of
the falls. Before shooting, I held the
shutter open for an eight-second
exposure to purposely blur the water.
The boulders remained sharp. That
contrast creates a mystical effect that
makes this scene so mesmerizing.

◀ **Fallen Birch, Upper Cascade
   Lake**

This photo accentuates the beauty of
spring in the Adirondacks, the stillness
of the lake, despite the pouring rain.
And the fallen tree made the shore area
even more interesting.

▶ **Looking Down a Cascade
   Mountain Waterfall**

On a spring walk in the pouring rain
(my kind of hiking weather) I came
across this waterfall. At the very top,
I perched my tripod on a ledge. I love
to imagine what it would be like to
follow the falling water, but the
photograph does that for me: It
captures the feeling of vulnerability,
that fear of "going over."

◀ **Junco in the Snow**
Juncos are commonly found in the Adirondack forest, especially during the winter season. I was lucky to capture this one just outside my tent one morning while camping.

◀ ◀ **Spring at Poke-O-Moonshine**

◀ Winter Views of the High Peaks from Blue Mountain

One clear, sunny winter morning after a snowstorm, I decided to head north. I knew I wanted evening light, so I left my home in New Paltz, New York in the morning, and drove three hours north to the Adirondacks.

When I reached the trailhead to Blue Mountain, there was much more snow than I had anticipated from watching the Weather Channel—at least two feet, and I had to break trail. It's great to have some fresh snow that obliterates all animal tracks, but this was too much of a good thing.

In order to reach the top of the mountain I had to hike in two miles and the sun set at 4 PM. I had arrived at 2:30. That hour and a half waiting for the sun to set seemed endless; the temperature was ten below zero without the windchill factor. The name Blue Mountain took on new meaning. I waited for the evening light to be just right; After I took this shot my camera literally froze, along with my fingers and toes. It couldn't have happened at a worse time as there was a magnificent moonrise just after the sun had set! So I ended up only watching this sight, unable to capture it, my frozen camera by my side.

HARDIE TRUESDALE   41

◀ Views from Giant Mountain

This photograph was shot on a hazy July day, and looking at it brings back memories of the pain endured to get it. I climbed Giant Mountain (4,627 feet) for the evening light, leaving for the summit at 4 PM. I told a friend it was a 2.5-mile hike in, and he said he'd go with me. However, it was a very steep climb, and about three-quarters of the way up he decided he couldn't make it to the top. I continued on. He surprised me, showing up at the summit around 6 PM, along with hundreds of blackflies. (Spring is the season in the Adirondacks when these noxious bugs hover around your head, fly into your ears, nose, and eyes . . . and bite.) Unfortunately I had forgotten my bug dope that day; I waited two hours before taking the evening photos and passed the time fending off those awful, fierce flies. By the time I took this photograph, I was covered with stinging bites.

▲ White Limbs, Giant's Washbowl—Detour off Giant Mountain Trail

On a search for the right shot, I've been described a resembling a wild animal stalking its prey. While getting ready to "attack" (get my shot), I feel a burst of energy and my pace picks up. I can sense the right place to take a photograph; in a way, I can smell it. I did lots of bushwacking around the pond to find these white limbs that sharply contrast with the dark trees in the distance. When I saw them, I knew that was just what I wanted.

▲ Blue Haze, High Peaks, as Seen from Giant Mountain Summit
Haze visually separates the mountains and creates depth in this shot, which is more like a painting than a photograph. I love to look out at these layers of mountains when I'm on a summit, especially in the summer, which was when this photograph was taken.

► Views of Chapel Pond from Giant Mountain

◄ ► Roaring Brook Falls on
the Trail up Giant Mountain

◄ Lake Colden on Ice

This photograph was taken between fall and winter, in mid-November to be precise. Contrary to popular thinking, you can photograph a scene without a lot of color and yet discover a richness of color when you see the photo itself, which is what happened here. One can find striking shades of color in any season, even November, traditionally considered a gray month!

I camped out the night before and carried 80 pounds of gear to Lake Colden. It was a crystal-clear evening—so quiet, so still, no wind. The lake had a thin glaze of ice on it, like a layer of glass. I watched the light diminish and photographed from where my lean-to was, while I cooked freeze-dried turkey for dinner. I usually shoot about a half-hour before sunset, which was when this photo was taken. Mount Colden, at 4,714 feet, is in the background. I love hiking in the transitional seasons; there usually are very few people around. I had seen one other person during the two days I was here for this hike. In the mountains, completely alone, I enjoyed the treat of absolute solitude.

▲ Frozen Deadfall, Lake Colden

One late-fall day, I spent several hours bushwacking around Lake Colden in order to find eye-catching deadfall for the foreground of a shot, so that Mount Colden would appear more interesting in the background.

The ice on the lake added a special dimension here. Carefully, I walked out on the ice and set up my tripod. Screws were attached to the feet of the tripod. The summit of a mountain is never a destination to me—it's the journey itself.

▲ **Spring Storm at Elk Lake—
Lightning Hill**

It was late April, and after snowing
all day the sky finally started to clear.
I wanted to capture evening light,
so I hiked a few miles to a cliff in
the Elk Lake Preserve and waited.
Suddenly, the sky opened up, and the
light traveled in and out of the clouds.

▲ **Cedar Roots, Eastern Shore
of Elk Lake**

This area in the Elk Lake Preserve,
with the twisted roots and dark woods,
reminded me of Mirkwoods
in J. R. R. Tolkien's *The Hobbit.*

▶ **Sunrise Mountain Summit,
Slabs and Clear Pond,
Elk Lake Preserve**

I waited more than two hours for the
sun to poke through the clouds. Why
this particular place? The cracks on the
summit rocks in the foreground actual-
ly drew my eye to the lake in the background. The Adirondacks' open rock,
moss-covered summits, unusual granite
formations, and ruggedness comple-
ment my compositions.

ADIRONDACK HIGH

◄ Balanced Boulder, Saddleback Mountain

This hike was a lesson in spring's arrival in the High Peaks. I hiked in to Johns Brook Lodge in mid-May with about 80 pounds of gear and food for five days. I arrived in the Adirondacks thinking the mountains would be enveloped in beautiful early-spring green. What I found instead was snow on the summits, with not even a hint of green. Off-season, Johns Brook Lodge provides bunks and a kitchen to cook meals. In season, there is a caretaker who prepares breakfast and dinner so you don't have to carry in food or cooking gear. May was still off-season, so I had to carry my own food, but the hike in does not gain much elevation and isn't very strenuous.

I spent two days waiting for summit weather, and on the third day I left the lodge at 5 AM for the summit of Gothics Mountain via the Ore Bed Trail. It turned out to be a brutal hike . . . like climbing up a muddy waterfall interlaced with patches of ice, making crampons a must. The first hour by headlamp was difficult, but I wanted to get to the summit as early as possible to see the best light. The Ore Bed Trail climbs to a saddle between Gothics and Saddleback Mountains.

From there, you climb steeply up the west face slabs via a series of cables. To complicate the journey, there was a thin layer of ice (known as verglas in the climbing world), making it necessary to take great care while hauling 50 pounds of camera gear up the mountain.

I arrived at the summit of Gothics at 9 AM, which was later than I had wanted, and found the melting snow an asset in that it created an interesting foreground affect.

I then climbed up Saddleback, where I found this precariously balanced boulder that helped balance the composition. Finally, I hiked back down the Ore Bed Trail to the Lodge

where I crawled back to bed and took some Advil to soothe my aching body.

I awoke to rain the next morning. When the sun came out in the late morning, I left for the summit of Big Slide Mountain. The views back toward Gothics were wonderful and gave me a feeling of remoteness. It was then that I realized I had not seen a single person (aside from the caretaker) at Johns Brook Lodge during the five days I spent there.

On the way down the mountain, I passed a beautiful series of waterfalls. Even though it was early, I realized once again that there is beauty in every season. Although I was extremely tired and sore as I hiked out to the car the following morning, I experienced the natural world in a way that drew me closer to the spirit of the Adirondacks.

◀ Second Pond Sunrise

I stopped along Route 3 on a crystal-clear, cold December morning on my way back from Ampersand Mountain, and waited about two hours for this shot. When the sun's rays hit the mist, I had what I wanted.

▲ Snow Squall, as Seen from Ampersand Mountain

The name for this peak comes from Ampersand Creek, so-named because its twists and turns cause it to resemble an ampersand, "&." Patiently I waited out a series of snow squalls so I could photograph from Ampersand Mountain. Finally, after five days, the weather cleared. In order to get the first morning light, I woke at 5 AM, arrived at the trail by 6:30 AM, and reached the summit (3,352 ft.) at 9 AM. It was a difficult, windy climb. As soon as I reached the top, the view became completely obliterated by both snow and clouds. The temperature was 15 degrees below zero, and the wind was howling. I lasted up there for 45 minutes, and was able to take two shots before the lens became covered with ice crystals and the camera literally froze. I hoped for the best, and this was the result.

Page 58: **Upper, Middle, and Lower Saranac Lakes, as Seen from Ampersand Mountain**
These are the views when there are no snow squalls!

Page 59: **Ampersand Lake and the High Peaks from Ampersand Mountain**

◄ **Night Views, Frozen Mirror Lake**
This photo was taken from my hotel room on the lake, and reveals a tamer side of the Adirondacks. I like the reflections of the lights in the lake made more interesting by frozen water merging with unfrozen water.

◄ **Green Boulder, Little Marcy on Mount Marcy**

No stunning views on my way up Mount Marcy, the highest mountain in the Adirondacks—just fog, and this solitary green boulder. This rock has endured millions of years despite the rugged conditions Mother Nature has doled out . . . centuries of snow, sleet, rain, wind, earthquakes. Yet here it stands alone. Such strength . . . and such delicate beauty.

▲ **From the Summit of Owls Head Mountain**

The hike to the summit of Owls Head Mountain, near Keene, New York is an easy one, popular for first-timers in the Adirondacks. I shot this photograph in an afternoon rainstorm. The fact that it was overcast may not be apparent, as I made sure there was little sky visible in the photo. The focus here is on other elements, particularly the green vegetation in the crack of the rock, a strong foreground image.

First Light and a Sunset, Lake George Narrows, as Seen from French Point Mountain

One spring evening I spent the night on French Point Mountain in order to shoot this sunset; then I eagerly anticipated the early morning light. The Lake George–Lake Champlain corridor is where much of the French and Indian Wars was bitterly fought, hence the name.

◄ Summit Grass, Algonquin Mountain

During the winter on this summit the wind was once so strong that I had to crawl around on my hands and knees. I waited for hours for it to stop so I could take a photograph. Such are the conditions that grasses must "weather" in order to survive—and it's miraculous that they do. The contrast of the soft brown grass works well against the solid mass of rock. Notice the "S" curve that leads the eye right to the mountain views in the distance.

► Fresh Snow, Algonquin Peak Trail

I love the peaceful softness of woods while snow is falling; here, a feeling of calmness and quiet pervades the scene. The foci here are the fallen tree and the colors of the coniferous trees. (Note the deep snow on the trail, which is why snowshoes are essential for winter hikes in the Adirondacks.)

▶ Hurricane Mountain—Sunny Summit Boulders

I snowshoed up this mountain with a few friends, but they left the summit soon after we arrived as it was much too cold for them. I stayed and took this shot. I love being above the tree-line; the snow freezes onto the trees and gives the landscape an other-worldly feeling.

▶ ▶ Whiteface Mountain, as Seen from Hurricane Mountain

HARDIE TRUESDALE 69

◀ ▶ Abandoned Buildings at Tahawus

No longer are there any mining opera-
tions at Tahawus (an Indian word that
means "cloud splitter") near the aban-
doned village of Adirondack (also
known as Upper Works), where these
buildings were photographed. Mining
flourished in this village from 1826—
when an Indian guide led a party of
settlers through Indian Pass to show
them a vein of iron ore—through the
mid-1850s. The operation started up
again during World War II when the
area became a source of titanium. In
1965 the village of Tahawus was moved
to accommodate a new excavation, and
the tailings "desert" that the road
crosses reached its present size.

▲ **Talus Cave on the Indian Pass
Trail, from the Upper Works**
I was attracted by the pattern of
tree roots introducing the cave, and
the light at the end of it, moving
your eye through the picture.

▼ ▶ **Wallface Mountain**
Alfred Billings Street, a nineteenth-
century explorer and author of
books on the Adirondacks, wrote
after climbing partway up the
mountain to view Indian Pass
from above: "After a few moments
of thus bracing my system and
recovering from the first sickening
shock, I again looked," he said.
"What a sight! Horrible and yet
sublimely beautiful—no, not
beautiful; scarce an element of
beauty there—all grandeur and
terror." He couldn't help but
conclude that the views were
simultaneously magnificent and
frightening!

► **The Great Range, as Seen from Mount Dix**

◄ **Evening Views from Mount Dix**

At 9 AM I began the 7.3-mile-hike to the Dix Mountain summit via Hunters Pass, planning to bivouac on the peak and take advantage of the evening light. Although I ditched the tent before starting out in order to eliminate weight, I still ended up carrying about seventy pounds of gear. I slogged through lots of mud on the trail, but the first five miles were relatively flat. Those last 2.3 miles seemed endless, with 2,000 feet of elevation gain in 2 miles. Finally, I reached the summit at 2 in the afternoon, and was revived by the stunning views to the southeast of Elk Lake and Clear Pond. The light was still too harsh, but I shot one image just in case the clouds moved in suddenly. Then, after several hours of waiting, I was rewarded with a beautiful evening light. This image was shot just before sunset. Several times during the night I woke up with painful leg cramps from hauling my gear up the mountain. Morning dawned cloudy, so the two-day trip up Dix gave me this one image and one of Dix Pond on the way out.

(Dix Mountain was named by Ebenezer Emmons in 1837 for John A. Dix, then secretary of state for Governor Marcy and later governor himself. Emmons was a college professor and geologist who led the party that made the first recorded ascent of Mount Marcy in 1837.)

Overleaf: **Dix Pond on the Hike Up Mount Dix**

◄ Storm at Round Pond,
   on the Mount Dix Trail,
   Adirondack Preserve

► Cliff, Avalanche Pass Trail
I had been searching for cliffs to
photograph; the distinctive patterns
of the rocks, as well as the contrast
between the trees and the cliffs, held
my attention. The photo was taken
from the southwest shore of
Avalanche Lake.

◄ **Fall Morning and Snag,
Heart Lake**

So much beauty is discovered
accidentally. While I was walking
around Heart Lake one rainy day,
I came across this fantastic snag.

► **Dead Paper Birch Pond,
in Autumn**

What attracted me here visually
was the silver-gray of the birches
in contrast to the bright colors of
autumn. Here, I broke one of my
own rules concerning composition—
the necessity of having a strong image
in the foreground—and it worked.

◄ **Lake George, as Seen from the Summit of Rogers Rock**

This hazy summer sunset shot came about because I was attracted to the long, finger-shaped peninsula known as French Point, which reaches out into Lake George. The haze helped to create the contrast between the starkness of the peninsula and the softness of the mountains in the background.

► **Colorful Canoes at Hickok's Boat Livery, Fish Creek Pond, Tupper Lake, New York**

◄ John Brown Historic Site

In 1849, abolitionist John Brown arrived in the Lake Placid area to assist local resident Gerrit Smith in creating a self-sufficient community for free blacks. Smith owned more than 100,000 acres, and he intended to give 40 acres to each homesteader. Unfortunately, the settlers weren't able to cope with the frigid winters and difficult farming conditions. Most left the area within a few years. Brown was executed on December 2, 1859, in Charlestown, Virginia, and a few weeks before his death interestingly observed: "Had I so interfered on behalf of the rich, the powerful, the intelligent, the so-called great—it would have been all right . . ."

In 1870 the property was purchased by a group of Brown's followers. Today the farmhouse and outbuildings are a New York State Historic Site, where Brown's "body lies a-mouldering in the grave," as in "The Battle Hymn of the Republic."

▼ Firewood, John Brown Farm

John Brown's farmstead near Lake Placid tells about the abolitionist's life in the Adirondacks during the mid-19th century. He came to the region to create a self-sufficient community for free blacks. Along with Gerrit Smith, who owned thousands of acres in the area, the two men encouraged ex-slaves to move north and gave them land to farm. Unprepared for the harsh climate and rugged mountain conditions, the experiment failed. Although Brown lived at the farm for only a few years, he is buried there.

Winter Sunset Over the Sentinel Range

A lot of luck is involved in capturing a sunset just right, but knowing where and when to go is essential. Just before this photo was taken, it had been snowing all day. About one hour before sunset, the sky had cleared. I knew the light would be particularly beautiful, as it often is after a winter storm. There was no time to hike a mountain. I recalled that there were open fields south of Lake Placid with views of the Sentinel Range. I looked behind me for sun, as I don't like to shoot into it. If the sun is at your back, everything you are looking out at is bathed in this beautiful evening light.

◄ Lake Placid Haze

This majestic view of Lake Placid can be seen from a car, on a hiking trail, or from a chairlift. What drew me here was the shape of the lake at this particular point . . . and the haze. Usually, I want a crystal-clear view when shooting from a mountain summit, but sometimes summer haze softens the harsh lines of the lake and mountains, and makes the view more ethereal. This image was taken from the summit of Whiteface Mountain (4,867 feet).

▲ Lake Placid, as Seen from the Summit of Whiteface Mountain

It's a wonderful feeling to be high up on a mountain summit. Unlike most mountaintops, the summit of Whiteface may be reached easily via chairlift or car, though the hike up is exceedingly long and difficult. This particular view of the lake attracted my attention due to the horseshoe shape created here by the peninsula. I omitted the foreground so that the drama of between the mountains and lake would predominate. At the time, an afternoon thunderstorm was rolling in. The haze accentuated the image, yet it also heightened the lines between the mountains, allowing for more detail and depth.

▲ ▶ Morning Mist, Mirror Lake,
Lake Placid

Granite Boulders and Moving Water, West Branch of the Ausable River

I was fascinated by the boulders gathered here and how they weren't washed downriver. Those rigid, solid, granite walls, the rushing water, and the rocks are all tied together in this composition. There's an interesting angle, almost triangular, in the foreground. Ironically, the mini-waterfall is the "anchor" of the photograph, even though it's flowing!

▲ High Falls, High Falls Gorge
On the road to Whiteface Mountain from Lake Placid.

▶ Storm at High Falls Gorge
This gorge is one of the few Adirondack attractions open to the public year-round. I prefer to photograph a gorge when skies are overcast. On this particular day a snowstorm raged. The road to the gorge was closed just after I passed through, so I had the entire place to myself. I was standing on a bridge, the waterfall behind me. Many people might have chosen to photograph the waterfall, but what attracted me was the fallen tree in the foreground and the falling snowflakes. When I keep an open mind and carefully observe the surroundings, I often end up shooting something I didn't anticipate. Surprisingly, the effect here turned out to be something like an Impressionist painting.

► Lake Tear of the Clouds

It was eerie up here in the mist as I stood alone looking out at what is hard to believe is the source of the Hudson River. Although it seems like nothing could survive in the stillness and stagnation here, life does exist. The lake is located at 4,346 feet in elevation, nestled between Mount Skylight and Mount Marcy; the closest access to the lake is over the summit of Mount Marcy.

Overleaf: **Opalescent Gorge Falls**

These falls were an unexpected treat on the third day of my Mount Marcy–Lake Tear of the Clouds hike, and the third day of constant rain. I couldn't escape the pervasive dampness, and hauling 70 pounds of gear over Mount Marcy with no views to photograph was disappointing. Waking up once again to pouring rain, I intended to hike out. I had no idea, while dropping down to the shores of Lake Colden along Opalescent Creek, of the magnificent scenery that awaited me: a magnificent gorge complete with waterfalls. Here the rain and mist were a bonus, creating a spiritual mood, a reward for sticking it out for days in such bad weather. After shooting these two images, I had to hike another seven miles before I could drive to Lake Placid and dry off.

◄ A Porch at Pinewood, a House in
Keene Valley

► Main Street, Saranac Lake

◄ **Blacksmith Shop**

Blacksmith shops, such as this one, were once essential parts of most Adirondack towns. In 1969 the Beaver Falls shop of George M. Bardo, which had been doing much the same work of blacksmithing and wagon repair for more than a century, was moved piece by piece and reassembled at the museum. The Adirondack Museum, Blue Mountain Lake, New York.

► **Bull Cottage**

Bull Cottage, built in 1891, is furnished with examples of the museum's renowned rustic furniture collection. Seen here are a white-and-yellow birch sideboard by Ernest Stowe made circa 1910, a mosaic twig corner cupboard made by Seth Pierce, circa 1885, and a pair of yellow birch rocking chairs made by Lee Fountain, circa 1920. The Adirondack Museum, Blue Mountain Lake, New York.

▲ **Adirondack Guideboat in Progress**
Boatbuilder Allison Warner built an
Adirondack guideboat in the traditional
fashion as part of the museum's perma-
nent exhibit, "Boats and Boating in the
Adirondacks, 1840–1940" during the
2003 and 2004 seasons. The boat is a
replica of one built in 1935 by John
Blanchard of Raquette Lake, also on
exhibit. (Distortion of the boat's shape in
this photograph is due to the use of a
wide-angle lens.) The Adirondack
Museum, Blue Mountain Lake, New York.

◀ **Adirondack Guideboat Exhibit**
The Adirondack Museum, Blue Mountain Lake, New York.

▲ **Classic Boat**
This boat, with its varnished finish and monogrammed decks, is a classic boat built around 1895 by George W. Smith of Long Lake for gentleman sportsman Alfred Thacher, a New York lawyer. (Distortion of the boat's shape, which appears in this photograph, is due to the use of a wide-angle lens.) The Adirondack Museum, Blue Mountain Lake, New York.

◀ **View of Islands, Blue Mountain Lake, as Seen from Castle Rock**

This hike on which this image was shot is approximately one mile from the Adirondack Museum and is often overlooked. Although the hike is short (only 3.5 miles round trip) and the last mile is quite steep, the views are well worth the effort.

▶ **Louisville Parlor Car**

The interior of the parlor car "Louisville" (first named the "Oriental") is virtually unchanged since it was first built for Austin Corbin, then president of the Long Island Railroad, by the Pullman Car Company in 1889–90. Private parlor cars like this one were a luxurious way for Gilded Age businessmen and their families to travel to their camps in the Adirondacks. The Adirondack Museum, Blue Mountain Lake, New York.

◄ Red Barn in a Snowstorm

There is a painterly feeling about this photograph, with its contrasts between the red of the barn, the yellows of the grasses, and stark white of the snow.

I had driven by this sturdy barn outside of Keene on many sunny days, but never stopped. Instead, I was moved to photograph the place in a snow squall, when the wind was howling and the temperature was in the single digits. Everything was soaked—the camera lenses had big chunks of snow on them. My tripod had to be held down so it wouldn't blow away. Yet the end result is this magical image . . . well worth the adventure I had to obtain it. The barn looks like such a warm, inviting place to go to escape the blizzard.

► Winter Shoreline, Schroon Lake, Eagle State Park, the Adirondacks

▲ Devil's Highway, the New Bobsled Run
with Four Turns, Verizon Sports Complex,
Lake Placid

▲ The 90- and 120-Meter Olympic Ski Jumps
Lake Placid hosted the Winter Olympic Games in
1932 and 1980, and the facilities there are currently
used for training by athletes throughout the world.

► Jumpers' View from the 90-Meter Ski Jump,
Olympic Training Center

◄ Morning Mist, Lake Harris

The campground at Lake Durant was full, so I moved on to Harris Lake State Campground, a place where I'd never been before. It was pouring, and I hoped the rain would clear and bring the morning mist. Early the next day, a few hundred feet from my campsite, I found this stunning image, complete with the cedar tree bathed in beautiful warm light and a boulder in the foreground. The stillness of the lake draped in mist created a wonderful atmospheric background. If I had stayed at Lake Durant as planned, this photograph never would have been taken.

► Birch Limb and Cliff Detail, Chapel Pond

◀ **Views of the Slides on Mount Dix from the Summit of Noonmark Mountain**

I arrived at the summit of Noonmark at noon; this pointed peak lies directly south of Keene Valley, and marks noon when the sun is directly overhead. The light at that time of day is usually far too harsh, but I arrived early because I knew a front was arriving that would interfere with decent evening light.

I spend a lot of time trying to figure out the weather so as to try to get the best light for a particular image. At times I work my tail off to arrive at a summit after hearing a promising forecast and find a great composition—only to find disappointment, such as when unwanted clouds roll in and white-out the horizon. Frustration is part of the work . . .

I sat and waited. Around 4 PM, white puffy clouds started sailing by, but the light was getting better, so I shot an image. Ultimately, I would have preferred to have waited for last light between 7 and 8 PM, but wasn't sure if the front would hold off that long. As expected, about 4:30 PM the clouds rolled in, and I knew my work was done, grateful I didn't have to wait three more hours for the light I wanted, and glad I had taken that sole photograph.

HARDIE TRUESDALE   115

◀ **Hudson River at the Upper**
Works Trailhead

▶ **Rock-Eating Tree,**
Owen Pond Trail

It's amazing how adaptive a tree can be;
here, this tree grew around rock to find
soil for its survival.